oing Bear Press

outh Huron Parkway, Suite 200
rbor, MI 48104
leepingbearpress.com

d and bound in the United States.

7 6

y of Congress Cataloging-in-Publication Data

ds, Pamela Duncan.
r Old Dominion : a Virginia alphabet / written by Pamela Duncan Edwards;
ted by Troy Howell.

978-1-58536-161-8
inia—Juvenile literature. 2. English language—Alphabet—Juvenile literature.
ell, Troy. II. Title.
.E24 2004
—dc22   2004006109

O is for Old Domi

A Virginia Alphabet

Written by Pamela Duncan Edwards and Illustrated by Tro

Text
Illus

All r
with
exce

Sle
2395
Ann
www

Prin

10 9

Libr

Edw
O is
illus
p. c
ISB
1. V
I. H
F22
975

For Billie Close, Sherry Wood, and Sue Henrich—
remembering the wonderful third grade 'Colonial Days!'

With love—

PAM

❀

To my Virginia friends

TROY

A is for Arlington
where the brave and the best
in old plantation grounds
forever lie at rest.

How would you feel if a cemetery suddenly appeared in your yard? This is what happened to Robert E. Lee, commander of the Confederates in the Civil War. Although he was anti-slavery and sympathetic to the Northern cause, Lee decided that, as a Virginian, he must support the South. The Union Army then confiscated Lee's home, Arlington House, near Washington, D.C. and used the grounds to bury Union solders. From these first graves grew Arlington National Cemetery.

Today it is the resting place of thousands of soldiers killed in combat and of many famous people, including President Kennedy and Christa McAuliffe, the teacher killed in the *Challenger* space shuttle explosion. One of the most moving sights is the Tomb of the Unknowns where unidentified soldiers from the two World Wars and the Korean War are buried. After Vietnam, an Unknown Soldier from that war was also placed there. However, in 1998 DNA testing identified the remains and he was returned to his family, leaving this part of the tomb empty.

You might think that after being born a slave, becoming the founder of a university couldn't happen. But this is the journey that Booker T. Washington took. He was born a slave in 1856 on a tobacco farm near Roanoke. Determined to educate himself after the Civil War gained freedom for slaves, Washington walked miles to enroll at the Hampton Institute, a college for African-Americans in the Tidewater area. He did so well at his studies that he was offered a teaching position. He went on to found the Tuskegee Institute (University) in Alabama. Washington encouraged African-Americans to learn skills that would enable them to farm their own land or start small businesses. He encouraged many Northern philanthropists to donate funds toward this goal. Some black leaders thought this was wrong and that African-Americans were setting their sights too low. But Washington believed in small steps at a time and Tuskegee flourished under his leadership. Today Booker T. Washington is respected as an important influence in the struggle for African-American education rights.

B is for Booker T. Washington,
who had a dream to fulfill,
that every African-American
should study and learn a skill.

Virginia has had three capitals since the colonists landed: Jamestown from 1607 to 1698, then Williamsburg until 1780, when the capital finally moved to Richmond. Thomas Jefferson designed the Capitol in a classical Roman style and many eighteenth century buildings still exist in Richmond. Both city and port thrived because of tobacco and cotton although, sadly, this encouraged Richmond to become a slave-trading center. Eight Civil War battles took place within and around Richmond, almost destroying it. The historic area known as The Fan houses statues of Confederate leaders Robert E. Lee, Thomas "Stonewall" Jackson, Jeb Stuart, and Jefferson Davis, but also of African-American tennis champion Arthur Ashe, of whom Richmond is justly proud. After the Civil War, Richmond rebuilt itself into a center of industry, banking, and finance.

Although a state, Virginia is known as a commonwealth. Early Virginians saw themselves and their appointed officials as working together for the common good. Today officials in Richmond still strive to make the Commonwealth of Virginia fair for all its citizens.

C is for our Capital,
a warm, enchanting place.
Virginians cherish Richmond
for her elegance and grace.

As spring returns to Virginia, the blossoms of the wild American dogwood appear in woods, valleys, and on hillsides. These are followed quickly by cultivated white and pink dogwoods in nurseries and gardens and the whole state seems to be covered by a mass of blossoms. The dogwood is not a big tree—it doesn't grow much higher than 30 feet. In fall, its dark green summer leaves turn red and small clusters of berries appear all over the tree. The dogwood was adopted as Virginia's state tree in 1956. The dogwood flower had already been designated state flower in 1918. So you can tell that Virginians really do love their dogwoods.

D is also for the state dog, the American foxhound. George Washington first brought these dogs into America from England to use for hunting. The foxhound can be any color, and is bright and friendly. It is medium-sized, growing to about 25 inches tall and has a hard, short coat. It was adopted as our state dog in 1966.

Dd

D is for the Dogwood tree
that welcomes springtime sun,
with bridal flowers of white or pink
that beckon summer, "Come."

E is for the Emancipation Oak
where they read out Lincoln's law,
saying slaves and their descendants
could walk through freedom's door.

Ee

The Emancipation Oak stands on the grounds of Hampton University, which was founded for the education of African-Americans after the Civil War. Hampton lies between Virginia Beach and Williamsburg in Virginia's Tidewater area. In 1863, two years before the Civil War ended, an historic event took place under this tree. The first reading of Lincoln's Emancipation Proclamation took place in the South when it was read to the area's black community. A marker near the university reads: "On the grounds of Hampton Institute is the tree under which Mary Peake taught children of former slaves." Mrs. Peake had secretly taught at her church before the Civil War. When the church burned, she held classes under the Emancipation Oak.

The National Geographic Society has named it one of the 10 Great Trees of the World and it is a proud reminder that everyone has the right to seek an education.

F is for the Four port cities
that lie on Hampton Roads,
where the U.S. Atlantic fleet is housed
and cargo ships unload.

The body of water where the James River meets the Chesapeake Bay and the surrounding area is known as Hampton Roads. Although there are many other cities in this region, **Chesapeake**, **Norfolk**, **Portsmouth**, and **Newport News**, with their industrial and port facilities, create one large port used by both the military and by civilian cargo ships.

Hampton Roads' harbor has been significant in Virginia since the colonists landed at nearby Cape Henry in 1607. A Civil War battle between the first ironclad ships, the Confederate *Merrimac* and the Union *Monitor*, took place there in 1862. During World War II it was a place from which many American troops set off for duty. Shipbuilding thrives in the area. Among other vessels, the Newport News Shipbuilding Company was responsible for building the nuclear-powered aircraft carrier USS *Nimitz*. Military presence is large in Hampton Roads where thousands of sailors and marines are stationed. Norfolk Naval Base and Naval Air Station form the world's largest naval base and the U.S. Atlantic fleet of submarines and surface ships is based here.

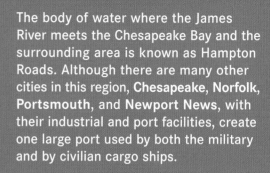

Ff

G is for George Washington,
    a leader very smart.
He was one of those who told King George,
"It's time for us to part."

Born in Virginia in 1732 into the upper class, George Washington wanted to join the Navy but his family objected. One day he surveyed the fields on his family's plantation, Mount Vernon, and enjoyed it so much that he decided to become a surveyor instead. Washington inherited Mount Vernon, and in 1759 he brought his bride, Martha Custis, to live there. He fought in the French and Indian War, gaining a reputation for courage, and in the Revolutionary War he became Commander-in-Chief of our army. At times the struggle seemed hopeless, but Washington urged perseverance; eventually the Americans were successful. Washington served eight years as our first president and earned the nickname 'Father of Our Country.'

In 1858 a group of women, known as the Mount Vernon Ladies, purchased and restored Mount Vernon. Today visitors enjoy seeing the house in which President and Mrs. Washington spent much of their daily lives.

H is for Patrick Henry,
who cried, "We should begin
demanding what is rightly ours,
freedom we must win."

Young Patrick Henry was the despair of his family. He tried farming and storekeeping but failed dismally. He married the first of two wives at 18, eventually producing 16 children with them. At 24 he suddenly pulled himself together and took the examination to become a lawyer. From that time, he embarked on an ever-increasing interest in politics. He is best remembered for impassioned revolutionary speeches inciting Americans to fight for rights: "Give me liberty, or give me death." He pressured the states to unite in the struggle against British tyranny, saying that the king was "a tyrant who forfeits the allegiance of his subjects." He stated, "I am not a Virginian, I am an American."

This spirited radical, with no time for 'aristocratic life' but with a gift for speech making, helped ignite the Revolutionary War. He became governor of Virginia three times before he died in 1799.

It is a mystery how the wild ponies arrived on Assateague (*Ass-a-teeg*) Island off Virginia's Eastern Shore. Some say their ancestors swam ashore from a sinking Spanish ship. We will never know. For most of the year the ponies enjoy the beaches of their home undisturbed but in July the traditional "Pony Swim" takes place. A number of ponies are encouraged to swim to the nearby island of Chincoteague. Here they are sold to new homes to be domesticated. Some people think it's wrong when these wild creatures lose their freedom. If their population went uncontrolled, however, their small island home could not hold the increasing number of ponies. If you read the book *Misty of Chincoteague* by Marguerite Henry, you will learn all about the life of one of these ponies.

I is also for the state insect, the tiger swallowtail butterfly. This yellow and black striped butterfly is seen everywhere in the state from spring to fall. It got the name swallowtail because the 'tails' on the back wingtips look like the tails of swallows.

Ii

I is for an Island
 where wild ponies roam.
Assateague is the place
 where they make their home.

In 1607 *Susan Constant, Godspeed,* and *Discovery* sailed to Virginia carrying over 100 Englishmen determined to found a new colony. The ships landed at the mouth of what they would name the James River. They considered settling on its banks, an area they called Cape Henry, but they decided to move upriver. A suitable area was found and named Jamestown, in honor of King James I who had supported the venture. However, conditions were terrible; heat, hunger, disease-carrying mosquitoes, and hostile Indians killed many. Also, the 'gentlemen' leaders were not used to work so the physical burden fell on the laborers.

Things improved when John Smith took over, declaring, "Those who don't work, don't eat." But following an accident, Smith returned to England and things worsened. More settlers came, more died, food began to run out, and 1609-1610 was known as 'the starving time.' Finally, fresh supplies, more settlers, and another governor arrived to give them hope. Although the settlers still faced many hardships, they began to believe that better days were ahead.

Jj

J is for Jamestown,
    where colonists, fearless to the core,
  landed in three sailing ships
upon Virginia's shore.

K k

K is for Kings Dominion,
with fantastic rides galore.
Up you whoosh,
down you swoosh,
and still you beg for more.

If you traveled between our nation's capital, Washington, D.C., and Richmond, the capital of Virginia, you might suddenly see a 332-foot Eiffel Tower! No, you haven't been 'beamed up' to Paris, France; you have simply reached Kings Dominion.

Over two million visitors come here each year to enjoy the incredible rides. They swoosh down water slides, fly upside-down hundreds of feet in the air, scream around hairpin bends on roller coasters, and eat 'foreign' food in the theme areas. King Charles II of England called the colony of Virginia his "Old Dominion." In 1975 the park's developers decided that Kings Dominion was a fine 'royal' name for this Virginia place of fun.

In 1878 Benton Stebbins, Andrew Campbell, and Campbell's nephew, Quint, were exploring near the town of Luray in the Shenandoah Valley at the foot of the Blue Ridge Mountains. Suddenly they broke through the entrance to the largest underground caves in the eastern United States.

Rocks, stalagmites rising from the ground, and stalactites hanging from the roof had formed amazing shapes such as: a sinking ship, an Arabian tent, a fish market. There was no end to the amazing configurations that met their eyes. Pools glistened in the light from their candles. They found a 'cathedral room' with an 'organ' that made music when tapped. Later, this was wired electronically and used to give 'organ' recitals. It became possible to marry in the cathedral room and have the wedding march played on this 'organ.' The discovery of the caves has delighted and amazed visitors for over a century.

L l

L is for Luray Caverns,
a fairyland underground,
where stalagmites and stalactites
in weird shapes are found.

M is for a house
that is called Monticello,
built by Thomas Jefferson,
a most inventive fellow.

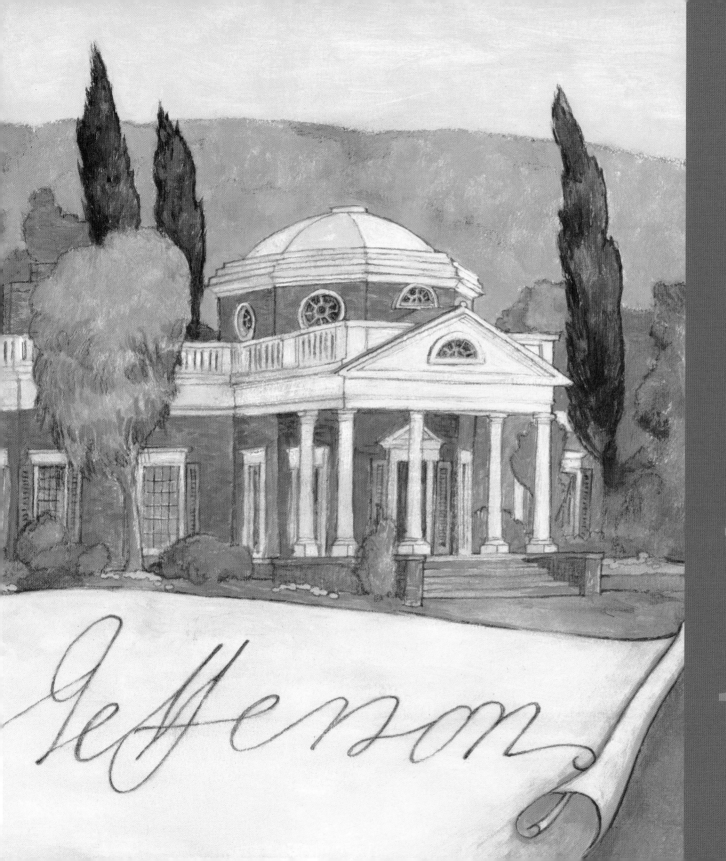

In 1768 Thomas Jefferson leveled ground on the top of a mountain and began building his dream house, Monticello. Four years later he and his bride Martha spent their first married days in the only finished part of the house. Fifteen years on, Jefferson had written the Declaration of Independence, the Revolutionary War had ended, Martha had died, and Jefferson had become ambassador to France. But he never forgot Monticello.

Over a period of 40 years Jefferson extended and altered his home where he brought up two daughters, and later entertained 12 grandchildren. This graduate of the College of William and Mary, lawyer, and self-taught architect was America's third president. He was also an inventor. His 7-day clock telling day and time; dumbwaiter moving wine up the side of the fireplace from the cellar; revolving door by which food magically appeared in the dining room; and 'copy machine' with two pens writing at the same time still amaze visitors from all over the world.

M
m

N is for Natural resources
like rich soil, rain, and good air.
Virginia is lucky to have these,
as well as a climate that's fair.

Aided by rainfall, climate, soil, and natural minerals, Virginia's four geographic regions are each economically important.

The wooded mountains of the **Allegheny Plateau** produce hardwood for furniture manufacture, and beef cattle and sheep graze on the pastures. The region is rich in coal deposits and natural gas. The **Ridge and Valley** region is home to beef and dairy cattle, horses, poultry, and apple and peach orchards. The hilly slopes are dotted with sheep, and limestone and sandstone are mined. The **Piedmont** region's clay soil is perfect for growing tobacco, one of Virginia's chief crops. Kyanite, slate, vermiculite, and crushed stone are found here. The lighter soil of the eastern **Tidewater** area is ideal for cotton, wheat, and corn. The famous Virginia peanuts grow here and often feed the pigs that produce the equally famous Virginia ham. Sand and gravel are extracted from this area. Virginia's part of the Chesapeake Bay is small but the seafood harvested there make it of great economic value.

When Charles I became King of England in 1625, he thought God had appointed him and he refused to listen to anything Parliament tried to say. In 1642 civil war erupted between his supporters and the parliamentarians. Sir William Berkeley became governor of Virginia in that year, an office he would hold on and off for 35 years. Berkeley was a great royalist and urged the colonists to support the king when this war broke out. Unfortunately for the king, the parliamentarians, or Roundheads, captured and executed him.

However, the English found they didn't enjoy being a republic after all. Following the death of Oliver Cromwell, the Roundhead leader, the old king's son, Charles II, was invited to return and in 1660 the monarchy was restored. The new king gave Virginia the nickname of "The Old Dominion" to show his gratitude for Governor Berkeley's and Virginia's support of the throne.

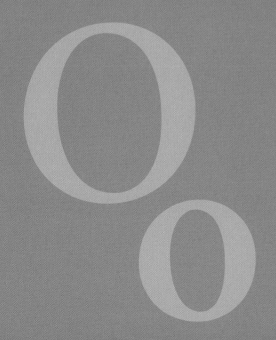

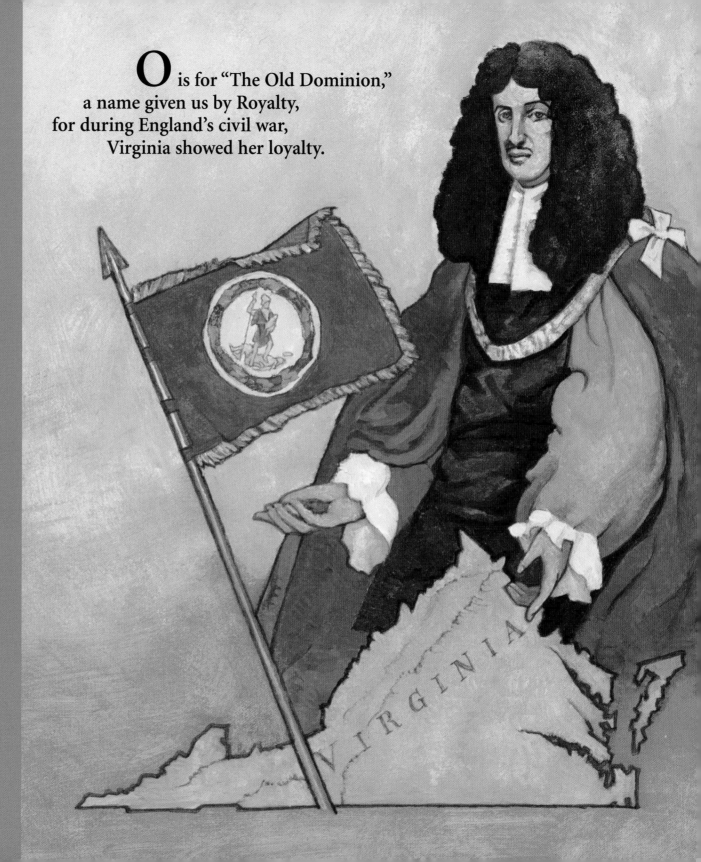

O is for "The Old Dominion,"
a name given us by Royalty,
for during England's civil war,
Virginia showed her loyalty.

P p

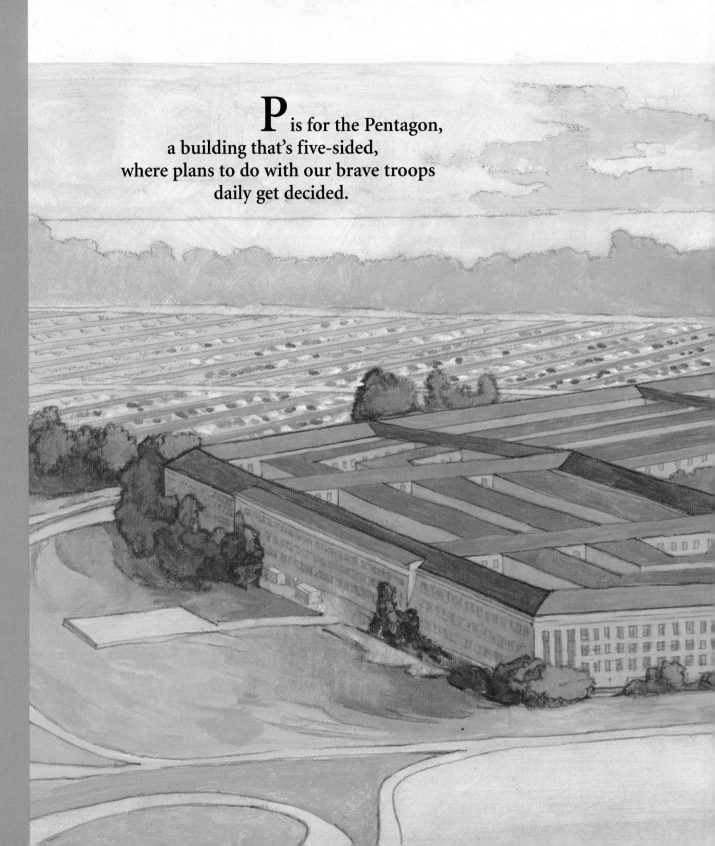

P is for the Pentagon,
a building that's five-sided,
where plans to do with our brave troops
daily get decided.

A pentagon means a shape with five sides. The Pentagon in Arlington is a huge five-sided building and is the headquarters of the United States Department of Defense. Thousands of people, military and civilian, work in one of the largest office buildings in the world. It is so big that there are 284 restrooms, 691 water fountains, and 4,200 clocks ticking away the workday. Although Pentagon mailmen use electric carts to drive the many miles of corridors, the building is so cleverly designed that it takes under 10 minutes to walk from one far place to another. The Pentagon, built during World War II (1939-45), allows all branches of the military to work from one site.

On September 11, 2001, terrorists flew a plane into the side of the Pentagon, devastating a large area and killing many people. Restoration of the building was put in place immediately and the devotion of Pentagon employees to maintaining their important work continues despite this tragedy.

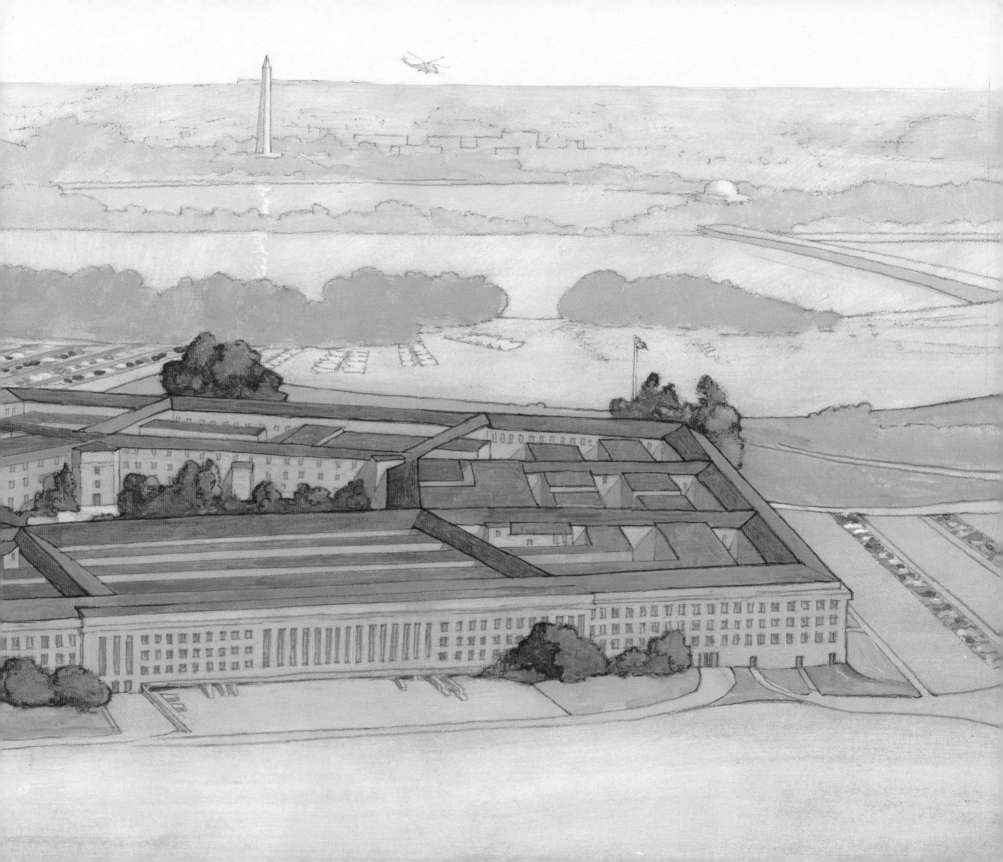

Sir Walter Raleigh, a great sixteenth century English explorer, named Virginia in honor of his English queen, Elizabeth I (reigned 1558–1603). Elizabeth never married. Her father, Henry VIII, executed her mother, Anne Boleyn, so perhaps Elizabeth didn't think marriage was such a good idea. Because she wouldn't take a husband, she was nicknamed 'The Virgin Queen.' Elizabeth was interested in exploration and allowed Raleigh to finance many expeditions to investigate founding a colony in the New World. Raleigh did not travel with these expeditions but it is due to him and Elizabeth's support that people learned more about this new land. Although the colonization didn't happen during Elizabeth's lifetime, she gave permission for the explored area to be called Virginia after her.

Elizabeth I never saw Virginia, of course, but in 1957 her namesake, Elizabeth II, visited to celebrate the 350th anniversary of the founding of Jamestown.

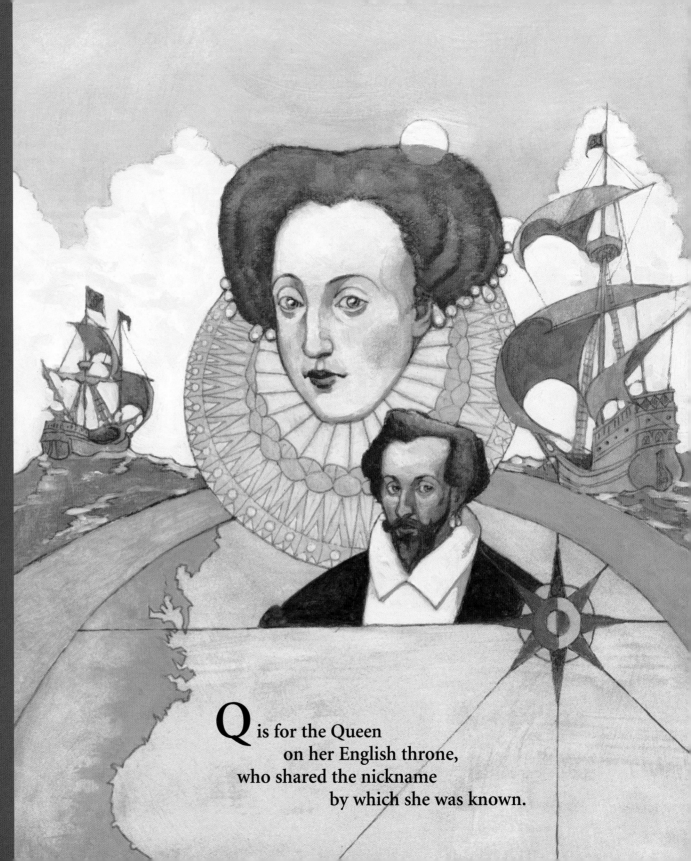

Q is for the Queen
        on her English throne,
who shared the nickname
        by which she was known.

Colonist John Rolfe was important to Virginia for two reasons: He discovered a moneymaking crop and he married Indian princess Pocahontas, famous for saving John Smith from execution by her father, Chief Powhatan. The colonists kidnapped Pocahontas in 1613, hoping to use her to bargain with Powhatan. However, she decided that she liked colonial life, changed her name to Rebecca, and married the widowed Rolfe.

Rolfe, realizing that Indian tobacco was harsh for English taste, obtained seeds from the Caribbean and produced a milder form. Soon the colonists were planting seeds in all available ground and exporting the harvests back to Europe. Tobacco farming had the effect of expanding the colony when the London Company in England advertised for new colonists to sail to Virginia, promising them land on which to cultivate tobacco. In turn, this brought the first slaves to the colony in 1619 after the new planters realized that they needed help to till their land. Eventually, slavery became one of the issues that started the Civil War. Descendants of Rolfe and Pocahontas are still living today.

R r

R is for John Rolfe,
who made Pocahontas his wife.
She changed her name to Rebecca
and enjoyed colonial life.

The London Co.

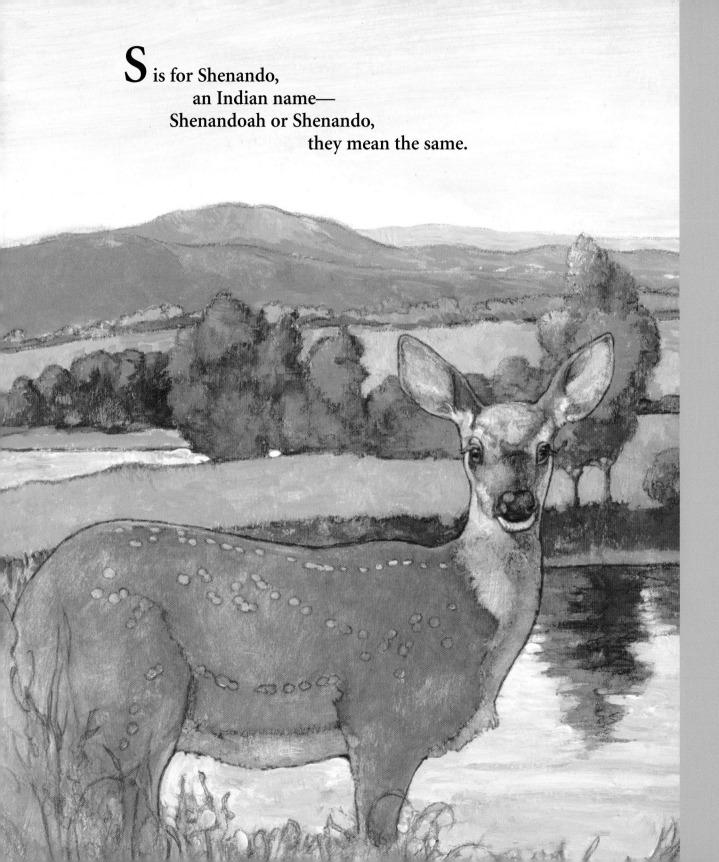

S is for Shenando,
    an Indian name—
Shenandoah or Shenando,
        they mean the same.

By the beginning of the eighteenth century, the coastal Virginia colony was overcrowded. In 1716 Lt. Governor Alexander Spotswood put together an expedition to explore further inland to the west. After a long journey over the Blue Ridge Mountains, the Spotswood expedition came upon a magnificent valley and river. Hearing the valley's Indian name, Shenando, meaning 'Daughter of the Stars,' Spotswood renamed both valley and river, Shenandoah. Rumors of fertile soil and beauty encouraged people to move there, and the area has played major roles in Virginian life ever since. Confederate General Thomas "Stonewall" Jackson, was born there, as was President Woodrow Wilson. During the Civil War, produce from the valley fed Confederate troops.

Nowadays, people hike, camp, and picnic in the valley or gaze down on its splendor as they drive the 105-mile Skyline Drive across the top of the mountains.

The Tidewater (coastal plain) is the low-lying area in the east where the Chesapeake Bay and four rivers, Potomac, York, James, and Rappahannock meet the Atlantic Ocean.

Over time, the rivers created peninsulas (necks). The area has many swamps and the biggest, the Great Dismal Swamp, is an animal and bird sanctuary. The "Historic Triangle" of Jamestown, Williamsburg, and Yorktown is situated in the Tidewater, as well as many other important cities, including the Hampton Roads' ports. Within the Tidewater lies the Eastern Shore peninsula, extending between the bay and ocean and shared by Delaware, Maryland, and Virginia. Also known as the Delmarva Peninsula, it is not attached to Virginia's mainland. To get there from Virginia, you have to go 17 miles across and through the longest bridge and tunnel drive in the world, the Chesapeake Bay Bridge-Tunnel. The Eastern Shore is a fruit and vegetable growing area and a stopping place for migrating birds. Assateague and Chincoteague Islands lie off the Eastern Shore, as does Tangier Island where the inhabitants still speak a form of seventeenth century English.

Tt

T is for Tidewater
    where bay and ocean both flow,
        along a coast that the colonists
            spied long ago.

Thomas Jefferson said his greatest accomplishment was the founding of the University of Virginia (UVA). In 1819 Jefferson drew up plans to build his university in Charlottesville in central Virginia, near his own house, Monticello. Jefferson followed Monticello's design, constructing a rotunda (a round building with a dome on top) based on the Pantheon in Rome. He planned a serpentine brick wall to snake between the buildings.

UVA is regarded as one of the best state universities in the United States. The campus has been designated by the United Nations as a site of worldwide importance. The athletic teams are all nicknamed the Cavaliers, in honor of Virginia's loyalty to King Charles I during England's civil war. Before the start of home football games, a "Cavalier," in seventeenth century costume, gallops his horse around the stadium to the cheers of students fortunate enough to attend the institution known throughout the state as Mr. Jefferson's University.

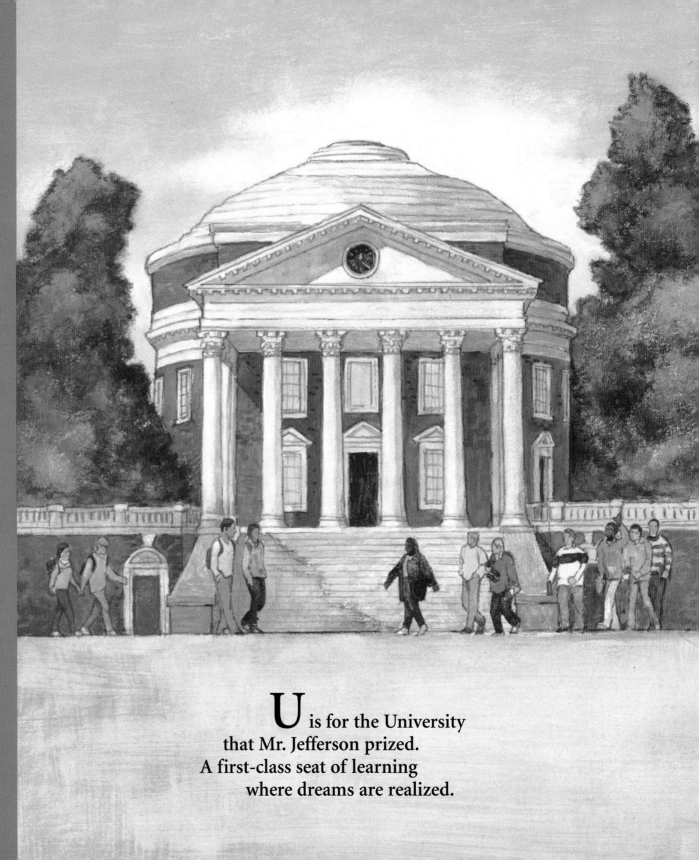

U is for the University
that Mr. Jefferson prized.
A first-class seat of learning
where dreams are realized.

Located in the Tidewater area and with eight miles of beautiful sand, Virginia Beach is one of the biggest resorts in the United States and welcomes millions of visitors each year. Virginia Beach has existed in some form since the colonists who founded Jamestown landed at nearby Cape Henry in 1607. There is a Cape Henry Memorial to remind visitors that here the colonists first set foot in the New World. In the 1700s Blackbeard the Pirate harassed ships and plundered cargoes along the shoreline.

When a railroad finally linked it to the city of Norfolk, Virginia Beach grew into today's playground. Modern families roller blade, bike, play miniature golf, swim, sunbathe, eat in wonderful restaurants, and visit historic sites such as the Adam Thoroughgood House. This may be the oldest brick colonial house still existing. Thoroughgood became rich by bringing over indentured servants to work in the new colony. Can you find Virginia Beach on the map?

V is for Virginia Beach
where people go for fun.
It's where they swim and sail their boats
and picnic in the sun.

W is for Williamsburg,
a colonial place,
where you might spy women
in long gowns and lace.

Where blacksmiths make horseshoes
and clockmakers mend clocks.
Where if you're naughty,
you're popped in the town stocks.

By 1699 the colonists had outgrown their first capital at Jamestown with its swampy surroundings and they decided to move to higher ground at Williamsburg, where the College of William and Mary had been founded six years earlier. The capital remained there until 1780 when it was finally transferred to Richmond. Williamsburg became neglected and shabby. In 1926 the minister of Bruton Church persuaded John D. Rockefeller, a multimillionaire, that Williamsburg history was worth preserving and a 30-year project of restoration and reconstruction began.

If you visit Williamsburg today, you step into the eighteenth century. Women wearing lace caps greet you; militiamen carrying muskets march in fife and drum parades; candle makers, wigmakers, silversmiths, and other 'colonial' craftsmen ply their trades. Reminders of colonial times are everywhere.

W
W

Virginia has produced many famous people. Eight presidents were born here—do you know who they were? "Stonewall" Jackson, famous for bravery during the first Civil War conflict, the Battle of Manassas, was a Virginian. Meriwether Lewis, from the explorer team of Lewis and Clark, came from our state. When L. Douglas Wilder became governor of Virginia, he was the first black American governor in history.

The sports and entertainment worlds have their heroes, too. Moses Malone was the first basketball player recruited from high school, and Arthur Ashe was the first African-American to win the U.S. Open and Wimbledon tennis championships. Brother and sister movie stars Warren Beatty and Shirley MacLaine, and jazz singer Ella Fitzgerald represent show business.

Cyrus McCormick invented a reaping machine and James Bonsack invented a cigarette-making machine. The list goes on and on. Can you find any other famous people who were born or lived in Virginia?

X
X

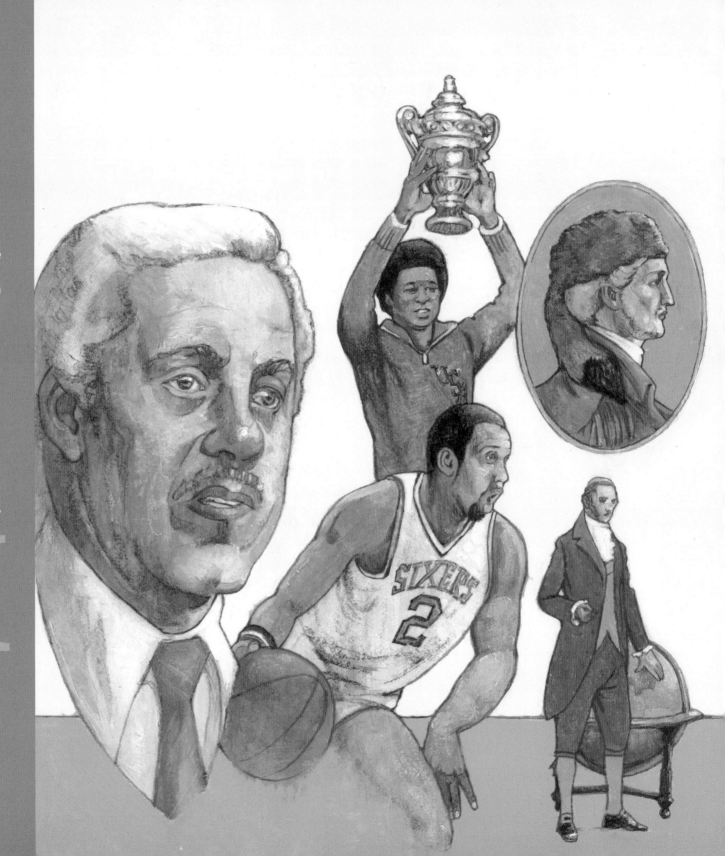

X is for eXamples
of folk from our great state.
Inventors, singers, movie stars,
as well as presidents—eight!

Y y

Y is for Yorktown,
a battle site,
that witnessed the Revolution's
final fight.

Yorktown, together with Jamestown and Williamsburg, forms part of a triangle in which many events in colonial history took place. After six long years of struggle in the Revolutionary War, Yorktown was the site of the battle that signaled the final outcome. In September 1781, 17,000 American and French soldiers faced about 8,000 British. The fight was hard but the British were eventually overcome, and on October 19 their commander, General Charles Cornwallis, surrendered to General George Washington.

Yorktown today proudly shows off its history. Cannon from the battle still stand on the battlefield and a monument commemorates the courage of those who helped to win American independence.

Zachary Taylor was born in Virginia but spent most of his young life elsewhere. He became a soldier, nicknamed "Old Rough and Ready" because of his casual ways. Early in his career he fought bravely in the Indian Wars and later was involved in the Mexican War (1846-48) where he became a military hero. In 1849 he became our 12th president, appealing to Northern voters as a soldier and to Southerners because he owned slaves. However, Taylor did not believe that slavery should be extended to any new states joining the Union. This infuriated the Southerners and North/South tensions increased although Taylor did everything in his power to find solutions to the problems.

Unfortunately, after being president for 16 months, he became ill on Independence Day and died shortly after. He would have been devastated to see the outbreak of the Civil War, 11 years later.

Z is for Zachary Taylor,
known as "Old Rough and Ready."
He was our twelfth president and
was brave and was steady.

Q & A The Old Dominion Way

1. Which military general had to choose whether to lead the North or South in the Civil War? Which side did he eventually lead?

2. Where would you find President John F. Kennedy's grave?

3. Who held classes for slaves underneath the branches of a tree?

4. Which president really wanted to be a sailor?

5. What famous Virginian said, "I am not a Virginian, I am an *American.*"?

6. Who was king when Jamestown was founded?

7. Which president was also an inventor?

8. What famous Virginia building was built during World War II?

9. Which war began and ended in Virginia?

10. Thomas Jefferson built a famous building using the plans to his own house. Where was that building?

11. Which president, born in Virginia, became ill on Independence Day and died shortly after?

12. What does the Native American word *Shenando* mean?

13. Who married a famous Indian princess and developed tobacco as a moneymaking crop?

14. What is the name of the Cape where the colonists who founded Virginia landed?

15. What famous Virginian was born a slave and eventually founded a university?

Answers

1. Robert E. Lee—He became leader of the Southern army.
2. Arlington Cemetery
3. Mary Peake
4. George Washington
5. Patrick Henry
6. King James I
7. Thomas Jefferson
8. The Pentagon
9. The Civil War: It began at Manassas and ended at Appomattox.
10. The University of Virginia
11. Zachary Taylor
12. Daughter of the Stars
13. John Rolphe
14. Cape Henry
15. Booker T. Washington

Pamela Duncan Edwards

Pamela Duncan Edwards came from England to live in Virginia over 20 years ago and fell in love with her new home. She was a children's librarian before becoming the author of more than 25 picture books. Pamela and her husband have two grown sons, a sweet daughter-in-law, and a wonderful grandson called Jackson, who all like to visit Virginia often. She thinks Virginia is the most beautiful state and hopes she will live there forever. Pamela makes her home in Vienna, Virginia.

Troy Howell

Artist Troy Howell has had a prolific career as a children's book illustrator with countless books to his credit, including *The Secret Garden*, *The Ugly Duckling*, and *Favorite Greek Myths*. He received his education from the Art Center School of Design in Pasadena, California, and the Illustrators' Workshops in New York. Troy lives in Fredericksburg, Virginia, with his wife, who is a native Virginian, and daughter.